Celebrity
Biographies

Selena Gomez

LATINA TV AND MOVIE STAR

BY ALLY AZZARELLI

Enslow Publishers, Inc.
40 Industrial Road
Box 398
Berkeley Heights, NJ 07922
USA
http://www.enslow.com

To Dominick Azzarelli

Library of Congress Cataloging-in-Publication Data:

Azzarelli, Ally.

  Selena Gomez : Latina TV and music star / by Ally Azzarelli.
      p. cm. — (Hot celebrity biographies)
  Includes index.
  Summary: "Read about Selena's early life, how she got started in acting, her band, and her future plans"—Provided by
    publisher.
  ISBN 978-0-7660-3875-2
  1. Gomez, Selena, 1992—Juvenile literature. 2. Actors—United States—Biography—Juvenile literature. 3. Singers—
    United States—Biography—Juvenile literature. I. Title.
  PN2287.G585A99 2011
  791.4302'8092—dc22
  [B]
                            2010048148
  Paperback ISBN: 978-1-59845-289-1

Printed in the United States of America

032012 Lake Book Manufacturing, Inc., Melrose Park, IL

10 9 8 7 6 5 4 3 2

To Our Readers: We have done our best to make sure all Internet addresses in this book were active and appropriate when we went to press. However, the author and the publisher have no control over and assume no liability for the material available on those Internet sites or on other Web sites they may link to. Any comments or suggestions can be sent by e-mail to comments@enslow.com or to the address on the back cover.

♻ Enslow Publishers, Inc., is committed to printing our books on recycled paper. The paper in every book contains 10% to 30% post-consumer waste (PCW). The cover board on the outside of each book contains 100% PCW. Our goal is to do our part to help young people and the environment too!

Photo Credits: AP Images/Charles Sykes, p. 16; AP Images/Chris Pizzello, pp. 1, 8, 10, 21, 34; AP Images/Evan Agostini. p. 9; AP Images/Gaas, p. 23; AP Images/Gus Ruelas, p. 29; AP Images/Koji Sashara, p. 41; AP Images/Litboy, pp. 6, 31; AP Images/Matt Saylcs, pp. 4, 15, 18; AP Images/Peter Kramer, p. 39; AP Images/Richard Drew, pp. 25, 26.

Cover Photo: AP Images/Chris Pizzello (Selena Gomez arrives at the Grammy Awards on February 13, 2011.)

Contents

Meet Selena!

Little kids often find one movie they enjoy so much, they can't stop watching it. "My favorite movie of all time is *The Wizard of Oz*," Selena told *US Weekly* magazine. "Judy Garland is the reason I wanted to become an actress." From the moment she saw the movie, Selena set out to reach her dream.

Selena Marie Gomez was born on July 22, 1992, to her mom, stage actress Amanda "Mandy," and dad, Ricardo. Selena is proudly named after the popular 1990s Mexican-American pop singer Selena. Sadly, the singer she was named after was murdered by her fan club president.

"My mom had me when she was 16," Selena told *J-14* magazine. "We lived paycheck to paycheck," Selena said about their hard times. Selena's parents split up when she was about five. The divorce wasn't easy for Selena. She and her mom lived in Grand Prairie, Texas, to be closer to her maternal grandmother.

◀ *Selena Gomez arrives at the People's Choice Awards in Los Angeles on January 5, 2011.*

▲ *Selena and her mother arrive at a* Teen Vogue *party in September 2008.*

Selena is a family girl. She is very close with her grandma and grandpa whom she calls "Nana" and "Papa." Her grandma helped raise her. She is very tight with her mom, who helps manage her career. When Selena was fourteen, her mom married Brian, who became Selena's stepdad.

Though she is very close with her stepdad, Selena still keeps in touch with her birth father. Born an only child, she loves her cousins and considers her friends and costars her siblings. Selena's mom helped inspire her to become an actress. "My mom did theater. I loved memorizing her lines with her and watching her rehearse. I told her that I wanted to do what she did, but on television."

FIRST ACTING GIG & BFF

Selena was bitten by the acting bug by about age seven. It was around this time in 1999, that she auditioned for the children's show *Barney & Friends*. The show was created and taped in the Dallas, Texas, area. Lucky for Selena, the show hired talented kids from nearby cities like Grand Prairie. "I was definitely nervous," Selena described her very first audition experience to PBS Kids. She didn't even have an agent at that time. "I was very shy when I was younger. I remember we had to wait in this line with

SELENA STATS

Full Name: Selena Marie Gomez

Namesake: Selena Quintanilla "Texas as a state is very proud of Selena. My dad and family loved her. So when my mother got pregnant with me, he wanted to name me Selena, after her. As I got older and could understand why I was named after her, I went to visit her grave and where she used to perform."

Nicknames: Sel and Selly

Birthday: July 22, 1992

Ethnicity: Mexican and Italian

Height: 5' 5"

Family: Dad, Ricardo Joel Gomez, and mom, Mandy Teefey, and stepdad, Brian Teefey. Selena is an only child.

You May Not Know . . . : Selena' stepfather, Brian, is starting to manage aspiring singers and actors. He discovered New Jersey YouTube singer/pianist Christina Grimmie and hooked her up with a slot on Selena's 2011 summer tour!

SELENA'S LOVES

Movies: *The Wizard of Oz* and *Alice in Wonderland*
Music: Fall Out Boy, Christina Aguilera, Paramore
Actress: Rachel McAdams
Actor: Johnny Depp
Celebrity Crush: Shia LaBeouf
Celebrity Friends: Justin Bieber, Taylor Lautner, Taylor Swift, Demi Lovato, and Nick Jonas
Foods: Pizza, mushrooms, jalapenos, Thanksgiving stuffing, shrimp, and pickles
Snacks: Rocky road ice cream, frozen yogurt from Pinkberry, and chocolate chip cookies
Hobbies: Skateboarding, surfing, singing
Color: Green

about 1400 other kids and I didn't know what I was doing. But then when I got to the audition, I realized it was just running lines, just like I always did with my mom. It was scary … but it was fun at the same time."

Selena met her BFF, fellow Texan Demi Lovato, at the *Barney & Friends* audition. They happened to be standing next to each other in the very long line. To pass the time, Selena asked Demi to sit and color with her. Demi told

People magazine, from that moment on, "Selena has been my best friend in the entire world." The girls were thrilled to both land an acting gig on *Barney & Friends*. Selena shined as little Gianna and Demi as Angela. "I learned everything from that show," Selena told the CBS *Early Show*. "It's such a wonderful memory to me. A lot of people would be embarrassed to say they were on Barney. I embrace the fact and I had such a wonderful time doing that show."

MEET HER BFF, DEMI LOVATO!

Full Name: Demetria Devonne "Demi" Lovato

Birthday: August 20, 1992

Siblings: Older sister, Dallas, and a younger half sister, Madison

Where You've Seen Demi: Camp Rock movies. She also starred as Sonny Munroe on *Sonny With a Chance*

Demi & Selena Projects: In addition to *Barney & Friends*, they starred in *Princess Protection Program* together and Selena also appeared on *Sonny With a Chance*

Common Bonds: Like her friend Selena, Demi is from Texas—as kids they lived 25 miles away from each other—and is both Mexican and Italian. Demi's and Selena's parents divorced when they were young. The girls are both singers/actresses. They were also homeschooled together because of their acting schedules.

From Barney to Beezus

After taping several episodes of *Barney & Friends*, it was time for Selena to move on. Because the show features young children, the cast continues to change throughout the seasons. "They said I was getting too old," Selena told *People* magazine. Selena continued to audition and landed a few TV commercials for Wal-Mart® and T.G.I. Friday's®. Soon came small acting parts in *Spy Kids 3-D: Game Over* and *Walker, Texas Ranger: Trial by Fire*.

By the time Selena turned ten, her career was about to take a more serious turn. She was discovered by Disney in a nationwide talent search. From there, Selena made a guest appearance as Gwen on an episode of the popular Disney Channel show *The Suite Life of Zack & Cody*. Soon Selena signed on to play a pop star named Mikayla on *Hannah Montana*.

FROM TEXAS TO TINSELTOWN

Selena was thrilled! She was meeting new friends and scoring steady work with Disney. In early 2007, Selena was cast as the main character, Alex Russo, on Disney Channel's series *Wizards of Waverly Place*. Alex and her two siblings are wizards in training. They live with their parents in New York City's Greenwich Village.

◀ *The cast of* Wizards of Waverly Place *celebrate with their Emmy awards for Outstanding Children's Program in 2009. From left to right are Jake T. Austin, Selena Gomez, Maria Canals Barrera, Jennifer Stone, and David Henrie.*

Selena was super excited about landing the role of Alex. However, she was sad to leave her friends and family in Texas to move to Los Angeles. "The biggest challenge was moving away from home, and at first, I didn't know how I was gonna do it," Selena told *Popstar* magazine. Her parents and Disney were very supportive and helped her with the big move.

"Once I came out to LA and started working, I adjusted a little bit but I'm still a Texas girl." Selena got used to life in LA by spending time with her *Wizards of Waverly Place* costars Jennifer Stone and Jake T. Austin—Jake even taught Selena how to surf! Jake plays her brother, Max, on the show and Jennifer portrays her best friend Harper. Selena also enjoyed visits home while the show wasn't taping. This gave her a chance to unwind and catch up with old friends.

RISING STAR

Selena continued to land more acting roles, and in March 2008 fans got the chance to hear Selena's voice as the mayor's 96 daughters in the animated movie *Horton Hears a Who!* starring Jim Carrey and Steve Carell. "I had never done animation," Selena told the *New York Daily News.* "I thought it would be cool to try something different." Because she spoke for so many different characters, Selena really got to put her voice to the test. "I had to change up my voice to do higher voices and then bring it down to do lower voices," she explained. A month later, Selena made *Forbes* magazine's "Eight Hot Kid Stars To Watch" describing the young actress as being "a multitalented teen."

In September 2008, Selena dazzled fans in the straight-to-DVD movie *Another Cinderella Story*. The romantic comedy is a modern-day Cinderella story. Selena played the role of Mary Santiago, a high school student who hopes to become a dancer. Selena took two months of dance classes to prepare for the part.

Another Cinderella Story also gave Selena a chance to show off her beautiful singing voice. She can be heard singing "Tell Me Something I Don't Know" and other tunes on the soundtrack. The director, Damon Santostefano, was so impressed with Selena, he told *New York Times* reporter Fred Topel, "She's not a little celebrity. She is actually a very, very talented actor who has really strong instincts and can sing, and can dance. She's a triple threat."

OH, THE RUMORS!

With everyone buzzing about Selena's success, headlines in the tabloids claimed she was set to become the next Miley Cyrus. In June 2008, the *New York Daily News* reported that Selena—who appears in a Jonas Brothers video—was dating Miley's ex Nick Jonas. This helped fuel rumors that Miley wasn't very fond of Selena. YouTube videos appeared of Miley and her friend Mandy supposedly imitating videos made by Selena and Demi Lovato. "I'm not here to replace anyone," Selena told UK's *Mirror*. "Miley is such a sweetheart. There is no feud, there's nothing going on."

Photos of Selena and Nick Jonas out and about appeared in magazines. Reporters hounded Selena to come clean about her relationship with Nick. A source close to Selena told *People* magazine, "They've been dating for months," to which a rep for the Jonas Brothers said, "They are not girlfriend and boyfriend. They're friends. All of the Jonas Brothers are friends with Selena." When confronted about the rumors on KIIS-FM by Ryan Seacrest, Selena said, "Well, he's an amazing guy. Anybody would be very lucky to be dating him."

Talk of Selena dating Justin Bieber began in the fall of 2010. By January 2011, the two were the focus of celebrity stories around the world. Photos were taken of them dining at a Philadelphia IHOP and smooching in St. Lucia. Talk show hosts, reporters, and fans have asked them about their relationship. Both Justin and Selena insist they are just very close, leaving it up to fans to wonder if they're really dating or not.

MANY MADE-FOR-TV MOVIES

By early summer 2009, Selena appeared alongside Demi Lovato in the Disney Channel movie *Princess Protection Program*. Demi's character, Princess Rosalinda aka "Rosie," enters a witness protection program. She also becomes best friends with a tomboy named Carter, played by Selena.

▶ In 2011, Selena Gomez was rumored to be dating Justin Bieber. Here, they get close at the 2010 MTV Video Music Awards.

Princess Protection Program was the third-highest premiere for a Disney Channel movie—watched by a whopping 8.5 million viewers. No wonder it won the 2009 Teen Choice Award for Choice Summer TV Movie. Selena herself won the Teen Choice Award for Choice Summer TV Star.

Later that summer, Selena starred in the made-for-TV film *Wizards of Waverly Place: The Movie.* Both films also gave Selena a chance to show off her singing voice again.

Selena kicked off a very busy 2009 by signing on to star in *Ramona and Beezus.* This movie version of the beloved children's book series by Beverly Cleary was Selena's first feature film. "I auditioned for the role [of Beezus] because I thought it was the perfect transition role," Selena told BuffaloNews.com. "I read the Ramona Quimby books in third and fourth grade ... I fell in love with the character Ramona. When I heard about this project, I reread all of them because I really wanted to do it and see who I could play."

◄*Selena Gomez and her little costar Joey King arrive at the premiere of* Ramona and Beezus *on July 20, 2010.*

Selena the Singer

In addition to being an accomplished actress, Selena is also popular for her sweet, upbeat voice. In July 2008, Selena signed her first record deal with Disney's Hollywood Records. Most of her made-for-TV movies feature songs by Selena. Her "Cruella de Vil" cover can be found on the *DisneyMania 6* album. She sings three songs on the *Another Cinderella Story* soundtrack. Her song "Fly to Your Heart" was featured in 2008's *Tinker Bell* movie. Her *Princess Protection Program* duet with Demi, "One and the Same," was included on the soundtrack.

Other songs by Selena include a cover of Pilot's 1974 song "Magic" (available on the *Wizards of Waverly Place* soundtrack). She also released a duet version of "Whoa Oh" with Forever the Sickest Kids on iTunes. "I work really hard on my music," Selena told reporters at the Kids' Choice Awards, "I really just want to make music that just makes people jump around and feel good." Her sold-out concerts really capture that jump-around, feel-good vibe.

SHE'S WITH THE BAND
In November of 2007, while chatting about her theme song for *Wizards of Waverly Place*, Selena told PBS Kids, "I've always said that I wanted to be in a band, so hopefully

◀ *Selena Gomez & the Scene arrive at the People's Choice Awards on January 5, 2011.*

when I start my music I'll be in a band, not just solo. You know like, me and four guys, something that's different and cool."

Then in the summer of 2008 it happened! Selena told MTV, "I'm going to be in a band. I'm not going to be a solo artist. I don't want my name attached to it. I will be singing, and I'm learning drums and playing electric guitar." After lots of auditions, the Scene was formed featuring Selena on lead vocals, Ethan Roberts on guitar, Joey Clement on bass, Greg Garman on drums, and Dane Forrest. When it came down to naming the group, Selena tweeted, "I named my band The Scene because a lot of people are making fun of me calling me a 'wanna be scene' so I thought I would poke fun of that."

The only difference in Selena's plan was her name had to be attached to the group due to a contract with her Hollywood Records label. So, the Scene became Selena Gomez & the Scene. Their first album, *Kiss & Tell*, was released on September 29, 2009. It debuted at number 9 on the Billboard charts and sold an impressive 66,000 copies the first week! *Kiss & Tell* featured a song Selena cowrote called "I Won't Apologize." The song was certified Gold by the RIAA—meaning it sold 500,000 copies in the United States.

To get fans pumped up for the release of her second studio album, *A Year Without Rain*, Selena & the Scene released

▲ *Selena and her band perform at the 2011 People's Choice Awards.*

their single "Round & Round" on June 18, 2010. The single debuted at number 24 on Billboard's Hot 100. A month later, on July 13, Selena Gomez & the Scene's tune "Live Like There's No Tomorrow" was released as a single, which would later appear on the *Ramona and Beezus* soundtrack.

The video for their second single, "A Year Without Rain," was released on September 3 and premiered after *Camp*

Rock 2: The Final Jam. Selena Gomez & the Scene have performed live on *Good Morning America*, MTV, and *The Ellen DeGeneres Show.*

Selena's band's second album, *A Year Without Rain,* was released on September 17, 2010, and debuted on the *Billboard* 200 at number 4. "It's kind of got a more feel-good dance beat and feel," Selena described to MTV. "It's different, kind of shows my growth of my music. I think if anything the lyrics are powerful, in a way." Excited about her 2010 tour and 2010 Jingle Ball concert appearance in New York City, Selena decided it was time to focus on her music and movie career. To do that, Selena told fans she would be wrapping up her final season of *Wizards of Waverly Place*. She has big plans for the future, including tours and albums.

FRIENDS IN THE BIZ

Selena's involvement in the music industry has helped introduce her to many other young singers. She's worked with the Jonas Brothers, Miley Cyrus, and Shakira. Selena has performed onstage with Justin Bieber at the Pop-Con in Long Island, New York, and has gotten supertight with Taylor Swift. Selena told *M Magazine*, "I feel like I've known Taylor Swift for ten years. Taylor Swift is so sweet." When stopped on the red carpet at the 2010 MTV Video Music Awards, Selena described Taylor as her best friend saying, "I'm here for her—I'm here to be her best friend."

Selena and Taylor became so close that rumors spread that Taylor was coming between Selena and Demi. In the winter of 2010, gossip Web sites began buzzing that the two old friends were no longer talking after a fan-recorded video hit the Internet. As Demi was leaving BBC Radio1 in London, fans approached her for autographs and photos. When a fan piped up asking how Selena was, Demi replied, "Ask Taylor!" Although Demi admitted to *J-14* that friendships and

▶ *Selena Gomez and Taylor Swift arrive at the premiere of* Another Cinderella Story.

people sometimes change, Web sites state the two have since put all the negativity aside and have revived their friendship.

SELENA THE BUSINESSWOMAN

In October 2008, Selena and her mom decided to start their own production company called July Moon Productions. Sometimes actors create their own production companies. This allows them more control over what movies they star in. Taylor Lautner and Drew Barrymore have their own production companies as well. July Moon Productions partnered with XYZ Films to finance the making of two Disney films.

You'd think making albums and movies and working with her own production company would give Selena plenty to do. Not so! The unstoppable young businesswoman released her hip, eco-friendly clothing line, Dream Out Loud by Selena Gomez, at Kmart in late summer of 2010. "It's crazy and so great," Selena said when the fashion line first came out. "All of my hard work has truly paid off, and I feel so happy. I've always wanted to do a line."

The reasonably-priced line features cute skirts, dresses, tops, shorts, jeans, and accessories. Most of the styles are similar to the outfits Selena would wear on *Wizards of Waverly Place*. "I didn't just want to slap my name on it," she admitted. "I wanted it to be real clothes that real people could wear. My mom wears some of my shirts.

I wanted to make a really good-quality clothing line…" And that she did thanks in part to designers Tony Melillo and Sandra Campos. Selena makes style suggestions. She also reviews and approves the fashion sketches and designs. Her clothes are cute, comfy, and low priced. They're perfect for her young fans.

▼ *On the show* Fox & Friends, *host Steve Doocy surprised Selena Gomez with a cake in honor of her 18th birthday.*

The Big Star With the Big Heart

Selena is one star with a huge heart. She does so much to help those in need. Selena's involved in so many causes—from UNICEF to UR Vote Counts. Selena told *Latina* magazine she was put on this earth, "to inspire someone and make a difference." Selena helps raise money and often acts as a spokesperson for charities. She's always giving back and hopes her fans will too. She helps ill and needy children. She promotes being kind to the environment. She spreads the word about safe driving. She raises money for education and much more.

"I think I've been blessed to have a voice," Selena said in New York's Moms and The City blog. "I've been able to have such incredible fans who usually range in age from 3 to 12. We're the next generation up, so whenever I get a chance to stand up for something I believe in and am able to give back, it really means a lot to me so, basically I just love to encourage other kids to help."

SELENA HELPS CHILDREN

Selena is the youngest-ever UNICEF ambassador. As a UNICEF ambassador, Selena uses her star power to raise

◀ *Selena hands out UNICEF trick-or-treat donation boxes to the crowd of the* Today *show in October 2009.*

money. She also helps spread the charity's message to her fans. UNICEF helps needy children in over 150 countries. The charity provides doctors, clean drinking water, food, and schooling.

UNICEF relies on generous donations. Their biggest fund-raiser happens on Halloween. UNICEF gives thousands of tiny cardboard cartons to trick-or-treaters. Children collect coins for the cause from neighbors and friends. "For American children and parents, Trick-or-Treat for UNICEF offers an impactful way to make a difference in the lives of vulnerable children," Selena said on the UNICEF Web site.

Selena has been involved with UNICEF for three years. She has even gone to Africa to see how the organization helps children. Selena has helped raise hundreds of thousands of dollars for the charity.

She took part in MTV's Hope for Haiti telethon and helped raise $65 million. The funds were split between UNICEF and other organizations. She often tweets about the cause and attends press events to spread the word. What's more, she donated the dress she wore in her "A Year Without Rain" music video to their charity auction. She donated proceeds from a concert and meet-and-greet to the cause.

▶ *Selena Gomez models the latest fashions at the 5th Annual St. Jude's Children's Hospital Runway for Life event.*

This pretty celeb helps out with a variety of kids' charities. In 2008, Selena joined Jennifer Love Hewitt, Hilary Duff, and other stars in Runway for Life. The event helped St. Jude's Children's Hospital raise over $1 million. A year later, Selena starred in special commercials for State Farm® Insurance, which aired on Disney Channel. In the ads, Selena warned teens about the dangers of talking on their cell phones while driving. "As much fun as driving can be," she told *People* magazine, "people need to learn what a big responsibility it is. You're never too young to learn about safe driving."

Selena also took part in Borden Milk advertisements. Like Selena, Borden Milk comes from Texas. Growing up in Texas, Selena says she drank lots of Borden. She also loved the milk's character, Elsie the cow. "I really wanted to do the Borden advertising campaign because it's kind of my job to be a role model," Selena said in a press statement about her role in the commercial. "For me I like to put positive things out there and try my hardest to educate kids on the importance of being healthy and being active. So being a part of the Borden campaign is an honor because it's kind of close to me."

SHE INSPIRES KIDS

During Barack Obama's presidential campaign, Selena became the national spokesperson for UR Vote Counts. Even though she was only sixteen at the time—not even old enough to vote—she toured 150 malls encouraging teens

Selena attends a UR Votes Count event in 2008.

MORE CHARITIES!

As part of OfficeMax's "A Day Made Better Program," Selena visited Charnock Elementary School in Los Angeles. She gave the students $1,000 worth of school supplies and a special award. Selena spent the day with the students and talked about giving back to others.

She has helped raise money for sick children. Selena joined Diddy and Christina Aguilera for Justin Timberlake and Friends, a Special Evening Benefiting Shriners Hospitals for Children.

Selena designed T-shirts for DoSomething.org. Proceeds went toward college scholarships for Latino students.

to learn more about the candidates. "Being a teen myself, I think it's really important we are educated on the issues that affect us all, so when we're eligible, we're fully prepared to take on one of our greatest privileges and responsibilities— voting," Selena told *Seventeen* magazine.

In 2009, Selena took part in Disney's Friends for Change. Friends for Change is an environmental campaign. The program encourages young fans to vote on which "green" programs Disney should invest in. Selena and her Disney buddies, Miley Cyrus, Demi Lovato, and the Jonas Brothers, recorded the tune "Send It On." This song helped raise funds for various eco-friendly charities. "Send It On" peaked at number 20 on the *Billboard* Hot 100.

Selena has also teamed up with DoSomething.org. This New York City-based nonprofit organization inspires and empowers teens to take action against animal cruelty in Puerto Rico. She posted the following on her MySpace blog:

> I'm honored to be the new ambassador for DoSomething. org! The last time I was in PR shooting Princess Protection Program we noticed all of these stray dogs and puppies. We ended up finding out that Puerto Rico has a 'dead dog beach'. It sounds worse than it is but people actually kill dogs for fun here ... This time around I'm teaming up with DoSomething.org and my mom, Brian, David, Jake, David D are all going to help out today along with some of my crew from set! We are spending the day feeding puppies, washing them and hanging out with them. After we spend the day with them we are sending these dogs to different places in the U.S — the no-kill dog shelters so they can find a home.

Staying Grounded

Selena's family and career seem most important to her. Selena is a spiritual person. She prays before every concert and TV show taping. She lives with her mom, stepdad, Brian, and five rescue dogs in a modest LA home. "Living with my mom and Brian helps me to be down-to-earth and to keep things real," Selena explained to Britain's *Daily Mail* newspaper. Her stepdad helps run her production company. He has taken her to press events and interviews since she was seven.

She went on to say, "I consult them about everything I do, especially because my mom is my manager. She's someone who loves me and wants the best for me. So even though I'm living this life and have been given such wonderful opportunities, I still have my parents with me to tell me 'no.'" Selena loves shopping, chatting, and dining out with her mom. "I definitely get more accomplished with my mom. I think we are similar in many ways," Selena told the British paper.

◀ *Selena Gomez hugs a fan at the 2010 Kids' Choice Awards.*

SELENA ON BEING LATINA

Being of Mexican heritage is something Selena has grown to become proud of, but like many kids, there were times she struggled with the idea of being different. "I wanted to be like my friends," she admitted to *Twist* magazine. "I hung out with girls who had blue eyes and blond hair and I thought, 'I want to look like them!' When I went to auditions, I'd be in a room with a lot of blond girls, and I always stood out."

Ironically, Selena believes that if not for her dark hair and Mexican roots, she may not have gotten certain acting roles. "I don't know if I would've had the opportunity to be on *Wizards of Waverly Place* if it weren't for my heritage," she said. It's important to love yourself, no matter what, and Selena sums that up perfectly, "I realize everybody wants what they don't have. But at the end of the day, what you have inside is much more beautiful than what's on the outside!"

Selena worked with DoSomething.org—a nonprofit organization that helps inspire young people to take action—and helped raise college funds for Latinos by designing special shirts. "Education is important, period." Selena said on the DoSomething.org Web site. "And for the Latino community, sometimes we get looked down on, when some of the smartest people are Latino . . . so I think we should just show everyone just how smart we are."

Selena has been featured on the cover of Mexican *Seventeen* and *Latina* magazines and continues to be a role model for young Latina women. She told *Latina* magazine, "I didn't even realize what a big deal it was to be Latin at first. But then one day being with my dad, it hit me: it's pretty neat to be Mexican. And there aren't enough Latinas in Hollywood—or there are, but they don't get the recognition. So to be able to come out here and use that, it's really a powerful thing."

POSITIVE ROLE MODEL

When Selena was turning eighteen, reporters wanted to know what her big plans were. How would she celebrate? She joked with them that she would just be hanging out with her family. She described her downtime as "boring" and uneventful—but that's how she likes it! "It's important to surround yourself with good people. My mom taught me that it's all about the people who you hang around with," Selena told ModernMom.com. "Luckily, I have an incredible family and great friends. My mom always tells me that my career is a privilege and I totally believe it is."

It is important for a youngster to have good role models. Selena has done an excellent job of making the right choices. The media loves to focus on young celebs and their drama. The press often tries to put a negative spin on things, giving performers a poor image. Almost every news story about Selena is positive. She also doesn't seem to judge others for making mistakes.

Selena herself has seen her famous friends go through rough patches. Demi had some personal issues become news in November 2010. To help Demi better deal with her problems, she entered a rehabilitation program. "I love Demi with my heart and wish her the best of luck and I definitely am standing by her side no matter what happens," Selena told the press.

Selena told a reporter for *Daily Mail* that her fans really keep her in check. She has to think about them before

► *Selena Gomez sings at the Z100 Jingle Ball concert at Madison Square Garden in New York on December 10, 2010.*

saying anything out of character. She remembers her fans before doing something she may regret later. "I would never, ever want them to be disappointed in me, because they are the reason I'm here. So I'm honestly just thankful that they've made me think about my decisions more."

SHE'S A PRIVATE PERSON

Selena prefers not to share too many details about her purity ring. She knows her fans look up to her. However, Selena thinks everyone needs to make her own choices. "I'd rather not talk about my purity ring because I never want to put any pressure on my fans, the ring is not important for anyone else but myself. But my ideal would be to not be known for who I'm dating, because eventually that's all you will be known for," Selena told the British newspaper *Daily Mail*.

Being in the public eye all of the time isn't always easy. Selena tries to keep a low profile. She wants the media to

focus on her projects, not her personal life. The young star went on to tell *Daily Mail*, "It's hard, because people are curious about who's in my life, but I want to be known for my work. And I never want to view myself as any different or any better than anyone else. If I wanna go eat at a little restaurant that isn't fancy, I'll do it. If I wanna go without make-up and not care what I look like, I will."

BRIGHT FUTURE

Making the transition from child actor to adult actor isn't easy. As Selena grows and moves away from younger roles, she wants to make the right career choices. Selena's role models are Nicole Kidman (she produced Selena's movie, *Monte Carlo*) and Canadian actress Rachel McAdams, from *The Notebook* and *Wedding Crashers*. "I would love to model my career after hers," Selena confessed to the *Herald Review*. "She's brilliant. She chooses smart roles, reinvents herself for every role. I admire that and hope I'm able to do that myself in my career."

Selena has said she would like to one day attend culinary (cooking) school. In fact, if she wasn't a successful star, she would like to become a chef. That sounds wonderful. However, at the moment Selena's plate seems full of movies, music, and fundraising. It's not easy to picture her having time to whip up fancy meals in a restaurant. However, her fans are sure to love her, wherever the future takes her.

Selena Gomez waves to fans at a special preview of Wizards of ▶ Waverly Place *on February 21, 2011.*

Timeline

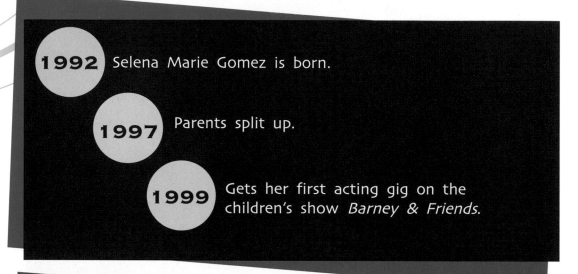

1992 Selena Marie Gomez is born.

1997 Parents split up.

1999 Gets her first acting gig on the children's show *Barney & Friends*.

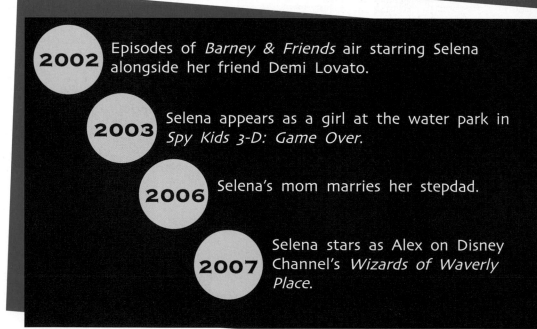

2002 Episodes of *Barney & Friends* air starring Selena alongside her friend Demi Lovato.

2003 Selena appears as a girl at the water park in *Spy Kids 3-D: Game Over*.

2006 Selena's mom marries her stepdad.

2007 Selena stars as Alex on Disney Channel's *Wizards of Waverly Place*.

2008 She signs a record deal with Hollywood Records.

2008 Rumors circulate that Selena is dating Nick Jonas and that she and Miley are rivals.

2008 She starts her own production company, July Moon Productions.

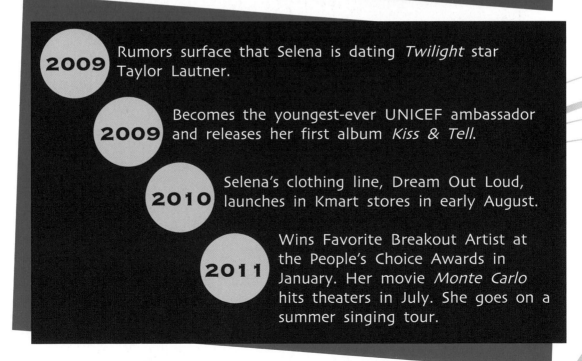

2009 Rumors surface that Selena is dating *Twilight* star Taylor Lautner.

2009 Becomes the youngest-ever UNICEF ambassador and releases her first album *Kiss & Tell*.

2010 Selena's clothing line, Dream Out Loud, launches in Kmart stores in early August.

2011 Wins Favorite Breakout Artist at the People's Choice Awards in January. Her movie *Monte Carlo* hits theaters in July. She goes on a summer singing tour.

Further Info

BOOKS

Brooks, Riley. *Selena Gomez* (All Access). New York: Scholastic, 2009.

Tieck, Sarah. *Selena Gomez* (Big Buddy Biographies). Edina, MN: ABDO Publishing, 2009.

Williams, Zella. *Selena Gomez: Actress and Singer*. New York: PowerKids Press, 2010.

INTERNET ADDRESSES

Official Facebook
http://www.facebook.com/Selena

Official MySpace
http://MySpace.com/SelenaGomez

Official Twitter
http://twitter.com/#!/selenagomez

Official Website
http://www.selenagomez.com

Filmography

2002-2003: *Barney & Friends* as Gianna, TV

2003: *Spy Kids 3-D: Game Over* as a girl at the water park, movie

2006: *Brain Zapped*, Emily Grace Garcia, TV

2006: *The Suite Life of Zack & Cody* as Gwen, TV

2007-2008: *Hannah Montana* as Mikayla, TV

2007-2011: *Wizards of Waverly Place*, Alex Russo, TV

2008: *Horton Hears a Who!* as 96 daughters, movie

2008: *Another Cinderella Story* as Mary Santiago, Straight-to-DVD movie

2008: Jonas Brothers video "Burnin' Up" as Nick's love interest, TV

2009: *Princess Protection Program* as Carter Mason, TV movie

2009: *Wizards of Waverly Place: The Movie*, TV movie

2009: *Sonny With a Chance* as herself, TV

2009: *The Suite Life on Deck* as Alex Russo, TV

2009: *Arthur and the Revenge of Maltazard* as Princess Selenia, movie

2010: *Ramona and Beezus* as Beatrice "Beezus" Quimby, movie

2011: *Monte Carlo* as Grace, movie

2013: *Thirteen Reasons Why*, as Hanna Baker, movie

Discography

SINGLES

2008: "Tell Me Something I Don't Know" also appears on soundtrack for *Another Cinderella Story*

2009: "Magic" (Originally by Pilot) also appears on soundtrack for *Wizards of Waverly Place*

2009: "Whoa Oh" (with Forever the Sickest Kids)

2009: "Send It On" (with Demi Lovato, Jonas Brothers, and Miley Cyrus)

2011: "Naturally"

2011: "Who Says"

ALBUMS

2009: *Wizards of Waverly Place*

2009: *Kiss & Tell*

2010: *A Year Without Rain*

2010: *A Year Without Rain: Deluxe Edition*

2011: *Shake It Up*

Glossary

accomplished—Highly skilled and talented.

advertising campaign—Commercials on the radio, tv, billboards, and more, promoting products or services.

audition—A test at which a performer or musician demonstrates his or her ability for a particular role.

culinary—Relating to cooking.

gig—A job.

inspire—Give one an idea.

ironically—Unexpected coincidence.

Latina—A woman of Latin-American or Spanish-speaking descent.

transition—A change.

triple threat—Someone who is an expert in three fields.

Index